# FINANCIAL
# RATIO
# ANALYSIS

I0423256

# A HANDY GUIDEBOOK

## CHARLES K. VANDYCK

**Foreword By: Kwamina B. Appiah- Mensah (Ph.D.)**

Editorial Advisor:  Natasha Lomotele Jones

Business Mentors:  Charles & Araba Vandyck
Makfritz Ventures, Ghana

Note for Librarians: A cataloguing record for this book is available from Library and Archives Canada at www.collectionscanada.ca/amicus/index-e.html
ISBN 1-4251-0526-2

**PUBLISHING**™
*Offices in Canada, USA, Ireland and UK*

**Book sales for North America and international:**
Trafford Publishing, 6E–2333 Government St.,
Victoria, BC  V8T 4P4  CANADA
phone 250 383 6864 (toll-free 1 888 232 4444)
fax 250 383 6804; email to orders@trafford.com
**Book sales in Europe:**
Trafford Publishing (UK) Limited, 9 Park End Street, 2nd Floor
Oxford, UK  OX1 1HH  UNITED KINGDOM
phone 44 (0)1865 722 113 (local rate 0845 230 9601)
facsimile 44 (0)1865 722 868; info.uk@trafford.com
**Order online at:**
trafford.com/06-2284

10  9  8  7  6  5  4  3  2  1

# Business Researcher

**Charles K. Vandyck** has a background in Business Administration with emphasis on Finance and Banking, Investments and Human Capital Development. He is an educator, researcher, poet and business facilitator.

Currently, he is a Senior Research Assistant at the Central University College, Accra, Ghana and a Facilitating Partner of TACIT TEAM. Tacit Team is an enterprise that is dedicated to providing Development, Educational and Management services in an innovative and effective manner.

Contact Address:

**Charles K. Vandyck**

**TACIT TEAM**

**P.O. Box GP 17951**

**Accra, Ghana**

**Phone: +233 243 128605-+233 244 789270**

**Email: tacitteam@freeghana.com, chuckvandyck@hotmail.com**

**chuckvandyck@freeghana.com**

**TACIT TEAM**

**Unleashing Productivity in Our Communities**

# Dedication

This book is dedicated to my beloved parents, **Charles & Araba Vandyck** and my brother and sister, **Johanna & George Vandyck**. Your immense love and support is humbling.

I would also like to dedicate this book to my **aunts**, **uncles** and **cousins**. You are all so lovely and I am glad you are a part of my amazing family.

Moreover, this book is dedicated to my grandmother **Mrs. Josephine Maria deGraft-Johnson**, for her unflinching love and unshakable prayers. I Love You.

Furthermore, I dedicate this book to Central University students, Alumni (especially the Class of **2002**) and all my friends. The world is ours!

Lastly, I would like to thank the Greatest Publishers, **Trafford Publishing Ltd**. You have made my dreams come true!!!

# Acknowledgement

I would like to take this opportunity to express my appreciation and thanks to my colleague and friend, **Christen M. Wadan**, who inspires and motivates me immensely.

Special appreciation also goes to **Alix & Anne Quashie**, **Samuel Moses Opoku-Agyemang**, **George Adjebeng**, **Ama Koomson**, **Splendy E. Macualey** and **Kofi Sarfo** for their contributions towards the enrichment of my life.

I would like to extend special appreciation to **K.B. Appiah-Mensah (PhD)** for conveying to me invaluable financial and operations management knowledge in college.

Lastly, I salute a woman who has inspired me to excel and work harder each day. **Natasha Lomotele Jones** thanks for your love, support and belief in me.

# Contents

## Section A: INTRODUCTION

# Section B: ANALYSIS

## Quantitative Ratio Analysis

## Qualitative Ratio Analysis

# Section C: CONCLUSION

## Vandyck's Financial Analysis Continuum

# Foreword

You are a business and finance student. You need speedy access to vital financial analysis information. And like a trainee accountant, law scholar, or any prospective business professional, you will have to master certain key techniques in order to stay on top of buzzing professional trends.

This handbook provides reliable and succinct data on the importance of ratio analysis. Its versatility and uniqueness is aptly explained. Ratio analysis is a significant technique that should be at the fingertips of prospective financial managers and business professionals.

I am convinced beyond reasonable doubt that this resource will help facilitate a thorough understanding of financial analysis and the drive to harness efficient and effective financial management in businesses.

This publication will be appreciated not only by examination participants at institutions of advanced learning but also by market professionals seeking an innovative guidebook on this highly important business subject.

**Kwamina .B. Appiah-Mensah, Ph.D.(Cand), School of Business, KWAME NKRUMAH UNIVERSITY OF SCIENCE AND TECHNOLOGY, GHANA, WEST AFRICA**

# SECTION

# A

# Introduction

# Financial Statement Analysis

## *Concept*

Financial statement analysis can be described as the process of establishing relationships between two or more variables and the discovery of changes and trends. It can be defined as the utilization of financial mathematical tools in order to derive economic conclusions. This includes details about monetary and percentage changes, trend percentages, component percentages and ratios.

It involves the examination of financial statements from the perspective of shareholders, investors, creditors and other stakeholders.

Ratio analysis is use of financial tools designed to determine relationships from a large quantum of quantitative data and disclosure notes. Financial statement analysis encompasses many procedures.

Comparative financial statements, trend percentages, common-size financial statements and ratio analysis are various financial ratio analysis procedures. Pertinent data is derived from financial reports by interpretation and application.

This data helps analysts ascertain relationships between variables, groups of variables and changes that have occurred.

Financial evaluation facilitates the strategic process in a company. This strategic process includes planning, evaluation and operations management.

Various business professionals and authors have defined financial evaluation in terms of a company's planned objective. In order to achieve key strategic financial objectives, data is derived from a company's financial statements. This data is used to determine the firm's debt position and flow of funds.

Traditionally, this versatile method is an aggregation of 4 core functions. These are screening, forecasting, diagnosis and evaluation.

These functions involve the selection of investment and merger candidates, determination of future financial conditions and consequences, assessment of corporate activities and the performance of managerial and business decisions.

It is important to note that financial outcomes cannot be evaluated in isolation. It is crucial that we develop appropriate comparisons to properly analyze the informational value of financial statements.

Determining an appropriate standard requires judgement. This is not an easy task. Financial statement analysis requires creative sophisticated skill and not a mechanical orientation. Financial statement analysis should be a proactive judgmental process.

## Importance

The primary reason for evaluating financial statements is to derive market value information from accounting data. Market information is more useful than accounting data.

In financial analysis, market value information is given precedence over accounting data. This data will be used to assess whether or not a company has performed well over a given period of time.

It also helps determine the value of profits that have been made by a company taking into cognizance the amount of money that had been invested into the business. A Company's future financial position can also be ascertained.

Financial statement analysis helps us determine whether a company is in a healthy short-term financial position, and a good long-term financial position. This is critical for growth and expansion decisions in every business.

Market-derived data has a variety of uses within and outside a specific business environment. This data can be used externally and internally. Two important external uses include corporate performance evaluation and strategic financial planning.

Internally, this data is used for credit management, competitor analysis, and new product development, acquisition and mergers. Financial analysis facilitates potent strategic decision-making.

# Tools and Techniques

## Year to Year Change Analysis

This tool measures the difference between the amount in a specific year and the base year. The percentage change is determined by dividing the amount of change between years by the amount for the base year.

This tool is used for comparison purposes over short periods of time. Usually within 1 to 2 years, a year to year change analysis is used.

This process is simple, manageable and can easily be understood when applied to many scenarios. It presents changes in absolute monetary amounts as well as in percentages. Its computation and interpretation is fairly straightforward.

# Trend Analysis

It is also known as the index-number trend analysis because it requires choosing a base year. It computes financial information over a given period of time to a base year.

Trend analysis facilitates the computation of data that covers a number of years. Trend percentages are computed and derived by a 4-step process.

This process includes selecting a base year or period, assigning a weight of 100% to the amounts appearing on the base year financial statements and expressing the corresponding amounts on the other years' financial statements as a percentage of the base year.

Finally, compute the percentages by dividing non-base year amounts and multiplying the result by 100. This tool is extremely important because it highlights a firm's extent and direction of change.

## Common-Size Financial Statement

It involves expressing each item on a specific statement as a percentage of key items on that statement. Each item on an income statement is stated as a percentage of net sales.

Common-size balance sheets state all amounts as a percentage of total assets or total equities. This statement measures the significance of the workings of various statements.

This tool is useful for inter-company and intra-company comparison. An inter-company comparison helps to determine differences in monetary structure and distribution.

Comparison with competitors and industrial averages is very critical because of its informational value.

An intra-company comparison helps to determine differences in amount structure and distribution over given periods of time. This helps financial managers make effective financing, investment, dividend and working capital decisions.

It is an important tool used in facilitating strategic financial objectives and goals. Common-size financial statements encourage effective and efficient financial decision-making in the corporate setting.

## Financial Ratio Analysis

This is the most popular and widely used tool of financial analysis. It involves the utilization of varying financial ratios in order to derive logical and coherent relationships that exist between operational variables in a firm's financial statements.

Financial data cannot be effectively analyzed without the use of financial ratios. A ratio highlights the relationship between two or more operational variables. It is a mathematical relationship between one quantity and another.

Ratio analysis helps decision-makers identify significant relationships and facilitates the comparison process between two enterprises.

It may be computed using information from one statement, such as the income statement or between different statements, such as the income statement and the balance sheet.

# Financial Ratio Analysis

## *Concept*

A ratio expresses a mathematical relationship between two quantities or variables. A ratio is calculated by dividing one number by another. To be meaningful, a ratio must refer to an economically significant relation.

It is an exhaustive examination of financial statements. This examination is executed by selecting, evaluating and interpreting ratios.

It is an analytical tool used to identify comparative relationships by measuring operational variables between two financial statement amounts. The function of this tool is often misunderstood.

Therefore its significance and importance is often hyped. The underpinning theory of ratio analysis is the provision of clues and symptoms of habitual conditions for the scrutiny of analysts.

If ratios are properly interpreted, it leads to the identification of areas, which will require further scrutiny. The analysis of ratios reveals significant relations and the bases of comparison in deriving trends and changes.

These trends and changes are usually difficult to detect by analyzing individual variables. This tool is futuristic in nature. It can be applied holistically, specifically and situational.

Financial ratios are defined according to their use and importance. No single ratio can be identified as appropriate to all scenarios. Each situation has its unique characteristics.

This requires the calculation of several ratios. It is important to note that financial outcomes cannot be evaluated in isolation. Therefore, we must develop appropriate comparisons to properly analyze their informational worth.

There are basically 7 categories of financial ratios. There are 5 primary ratios and 2 secondary ratios. The primary ratios are the principal and the most common measurements of financial health.

Secondary financial ratios can be characterized as support and utility ratios. Both categories of ratios are extremely important and useful for efficient, effective and timely financial management.

Primary financial ratios include short-term solvency or liquidity ratios, asset management or turnover ratios, long-term solvency or debt management ratios, profitability ratios and stock market measures or ratios.

Secondary financial ratios include corporate growth ratios and internal and sustainable growth ratios.

## Importance

Ratio analysis is versatile and unique. This tool is interdisciplinary in nature and contributes extensively towards the determination of significant relationships between two or more mathematical quantities.

Most ratios are easy to calculate and interpret. The process of evaluation and interpretation of data provides important information for strategic financial management purposes.

Ratio analysis helps gain insight into the true nature of a firm's financial potency and future outlook. This analysis helps determine the leverage situation of a firm.

That is, the relationship between its equity and debt. Equity and debt are the two options available for business entities in terms of financial inflows.

Every firm tries to avoid transforming itself into a highly leveraged company. This is a situation where debt exceeds equity.

A critical and exhaustive study into financial ratios is seriously needed because of its appeal, popularity and simplicity.

It may not provide glaring answers for decision making but it is the most important part of the transformation process that links interpretation to application. Informed application leads to growth and development in business entities.

# Corporate Uses

## Performance Evaluation

Information obtained from financial statements using ratios is primarily used to undertake performance evaluation. Performance evaluation is a process that seeks to determine the extent or degree of a firm's growth and development from the input made by management.

The Chief Executive Officers of businesses are frequently evaluated. They are compensated based on the performance of certain ratios like the gross profit margin, return on investment, return on equity and the corporate growth ratios.

## Strategic Financial Planning

Ratio analysis provides market information that can be utilized during the process of strategic financial planning and growth. Historical financial statement information is very useful for generating projections about the future and for checking the true nature of financial projections.

Strategic financial planning is an important process in corporate governance. Ratio analysis facilitates strategic financial planning by providing data on the liquidity, asset management, and the debt profile of a company. This information will be used to achieve key financial targets and objectives.

## Credit Management

This technique is an effective credit management tool. It helps in the formulation and execution of credit management decisions.

An individual or an organization that is considering contracting a loan needs to know whether the borrower is likely to be able to repay the loan and its interest. Information from ratio analysis can be used to evaluate suppliers.

Suppliers use financial statements before deciding to extend credit facilities. Customers with large bargaining influence use this information to decide if a specific company is likely to be around in the future.

Information extracted from a firm's financial statements can give a clear picture of the status of a company's profitability and efficiency of its business operations.

# Other Uses

## Competitor Analysis

Ratio analysis helps facilitate the process of competitor analysis. It is important to know whether a competitor has the funds to execute a similar new product development you are thinking about launching.

It is strategically prudent for every organization to keep a close eye on its competitors. It is also important to assess a competitor's financial capabilities during the course of its business life.

## Mergers and Acquisitions

An important peripheral use of financial ratio analysis is in the area of acquisition and mergers.

An investor may be thinking of contracting or assuming or acquiring possession of an asset or company.

Financial statement information would be an important aspect in terms of the identification of potential targets and the significance of the existing offer.

Ratio analysis is an invaluable guide for the decision-maker in deciding on the merits and demerits of a merger.

This is more pronounced in cases where the authenticity of a unification of two or more entities is being challenged.

# Limitations

## Accounting Information

Firms use different accounting policies. This reality makes it difficult to compare firms with other firms in their industry. Inter-company comparisons are seriously affected by this situation. Accounts are usually prepared under the historical cost convention.

When an asset is valued at a depreciated historical cost, a business may choose not to revalue its assets. This is because by so doing the depreciation charge is going to be high and this will result in lower profit.

Most firms practice creative accounting. This is the process of propping up a company's financial performance. This exercise paints a misleading picture to the users of the accounts.

Some authors have described creative accounting as accounting and financial reporting practices that convey a circumstance or position that is misleading or illusory. It creates a position of profitability and liquidity that may not be totally valid.

## Value of Information

It is important to note that ratios are not definitive measures. They need to be interpreted carefully. Ratios provide clues about the company's performance and financial position.

On their own, they cannot show whether performance is good or bad. They require qualitative information for an informed analysis to be made.

Information highlighted in financial statements is likely to be at least several months out of date. It does not give a realistic picture of the firm's current financial position.

Most accounting bodies in the world recommend businesses to use historical cost accounting. When this convention is used, asset valuations in the balance sheet could be misleading.

Ratios are usually based on financial statements that are of varying accounting records. The process of summarization may lead to pertinent information being left out which could have been relevant to the users of accounts. The ratios may not be a true reflection of the overall year's results.

It is difficult to ascertain whether an outcome of a ratio is good or bad. For instance a high current ratio may indicate a strong liquidity position, which is good. It may also indicate excess cash which is harmful.

# Comparison of Performance over Time

Inflation affects comparisons made over a period of time. It renders ratios misleading, as financial figures will not be within the same levels of purchasing power.

Changes in results over time may show as that the enterprise has improved its performance and position. This situation may not be the truth after adjusting for inflationary changes. A different picture could be revealed.

When comparing performance over time, there is the need to consider the changes in technology. For ratios to be more meaningful, the firm should compare its results with another firm that is as technologically enhanced. This promotes efficiency and effectiveness in corporate strata.

Rampant changes in accounting policy may affect the comparison of results between different accounting years. Management may be able to manipulate the results through changes in accounting policies.

This is done to avoid the effects of an old accounting policy or gain the effects of a new one. It is likely to be executed in a sensitive period when business profits are declining.

Any change in recognized accounting standards would affect the reporting of the finances of an enterprise and its comparative rank over a number of years. Accounting standards are conventional ways of recognizing, measuring and presenting financial dealings.

Some financial statements are based on year-end results. Businesses that are seasonal often choose the best time to produce financial statements so as to portray better results.

This may misrepresent the actual financial standing of the specific business. For example in Ghana, cocoa-growing companies may portray good results if accounts are prepared during the selling season.

During the selling season, the business would have appreciably good inventory levels, receivables and bank balances. In the planting season the enterprise would have a lot of liabilities through the purchase of farm implements. They will most probably have low cash balances.

# Inter-Firm Comparison

Firms may deal in the same products or services. They may be in the same industry but have different financial and business risk profiles. A Company may be able to access bank loans at reduced rates even though its operations are highly indebted.

Another firm may not be successful in obtaining low rates even though it is operating at a low debt level. This company may look likely to obtain the loan but a lot depends on its risk structure.

Companies may have contrasted capital structures. This makes it difficult to analyze comparisons of performance when one could be highly leveraged and the other low geared. A prudent decision would be a difficult and seemingly impossible outcome.

The influence and impact of government incentives to various enterprises makes inter-company comparison very difficult. When a company in a specific industry obtains a tax holiday while the other does not, comparing the performance of these entities may be open to doubt.

Window dressing is commonly practiced by entities to get out of sticky positions at the end of an accounting year in order to improve perceptions.

For instance a firm can access a loan on a 3-year basis at the end of a specific financial year and pay off the loan exactly a month afterwards.

This seemingly improves the current financial position and makes the base year balance sheet look good. However the purported improvement is a mirage.

Ratio analysis is generally very useful but analysts should be aware of the above-numerated problems and make necessary adjustments when it falls due.

Ratio analysis conducted in a rigid manner is fleeting, but if used intelligently with good judgement, it can provide useful insight into a firm's operations.

# The Annual Report

## *Concept*

The annual report is an annual legal statement that a business produces for its shareholders' in order to present its annual accounts at its annual general meeting.

The report normally includes a profit and loss statement or income statement, balance sheet, statement of retained earnings, statement of cash flows, notes to accounts and an auditors' report. It is usually a smooth, colourful and glossy publication.

It can also be described as a document detailing the business activity of a company over the previous year and an aggregation of 3 main financial statements, income statement, statement of cash flows and balance sheet.

Corporate entities that have shareholders must prepare an annual report and make it available to the companies shareholders.

The basic purpose of an annual report is to let the shareholders know how the company is doing. The annual report contains information such as indispensable financial statements, management's opinion of the past years operations and the enterprises future prospects.

This report is prepared yearly and is published by a public company, detailing a wide range of financial information including its balance sheet, income statement and other pertinent information about its operations. It is also referred to as a stockholders' report.

It is an audited corporate document that details the business activity and financial status of a public company over the previous year.

The Securities and Exchange Commission (SEC) requires all state companies to furnish an annual report to shareholders at the end of each fiscal year.

Each report contains the 3 main financial statements. Namely, the income statement, cash flow statement and balance sheet as well as a host of other company related data.

Annual reports are important primary documents. That is, they are original sources of corporate data revealing the socio-cultural and economic history of s specific company.

Information derived from these reports can be used to devise communication strategies and design. Electronic and standardized corporate financial data provides insight into communication and design strategies.

This information also highlights the expenditure patterns of the specific entity. This helps in identifying the importance that is given to certain expenses and its attendant impact on the company's performance.

For an educated and informed investor, corporate annual reports are the most important research material. Annual reports help investors manage and compute performance trends on a yearly basis.

## Balance Sheet

A balance sheet is a record of the financial position of an enterprise on a particular date by listing its assets and the claims against those assets. It is a telescopic view of a business' financial condition at a specific moment in time, usually at the close of an accounting period.

It comprises of assets, liabilities and stockholders equity. Assets and liabilities are divided into short and long-term obligations. At any given time assets must equal liabilities plus owners' equity. An asset is anything a business owns that has monetary value. Liabilities are claims of creditors against the assets of the business.

A balance sheet can also be defined as the statement of a particular time that highlights the debt and assets of an enterprise. It is usually prepared on a monthly, quarterly or yearly basis. In addition, it is also prepared when the business is sold.

The purpose of this statement is to portray the overall performance of the enterprise. It facilitates the process of assessing strengths and capabilities of a business.

It can identify and analyze trends, particularly in the area of receivables and payables. It is one the most basic elements in the provision of financial reporting to potential lenders such as Banks, Investors and Merchants.

## Features of a Balance Sheet

## Assets

Assets are subdivided into current and long-term assets. This division shows the distinction between the most liquid and the least. Cash is considered the most liquid of all assets. Long-term assets such as machinery are less likely to convert easily and quickly into cash.

Current Assets are any assets that can easily be converted into cash within 1 calendar year. Examples of current assets are money market accounts and notes receivables that are due within a year's time. Cash is money available immediately. It is the most liquid of all short-term assets.

Debtors or Accounts receivables are money owed to the business for purchases made by customers, suppliers and other vendors. Notes receivables that fall due within a year are current assets. Notes that cannot be collected within a year should be considered long-term assets.

Fixed Assets include tangible wares like land, buildings, machinery and vehicles that are used for the effective management of the business. Land is a fixed asset but unlike other fixed assets, it does not depreciate. This is because it is considered as an asset that never wears out.

Buildings are fixed assets and they depreciate over time. Office equipment like photo copiers, scanners printers and personal computers are all considered to be fixed assets. Total assets encompass the total monetary value of all short-term and long-term assets of the enterprise.

## Liabilities and Owners' Equity

Liabilities and Owners' Equity includes all debts and obligations owed by the business to outside creditors, finance houses or banks that are payable within one year plus the owners' equity.

This side of the balance sheet is referred to us liabilities. Accounts payable constitutes all short-term obligations owed by your enterprise to creditors, suppliers and other lenders.

Notes payable represents money owed on a short-term collection phase of one year or less. It may include bank notes, mortgage obligations, and vehicle payments among other things.

Accrued payroll and withholding includes any earned wages or withholding that are owed to or for employees but have not yet been paid.

Total current liabilities are the aggregation of all current liabilities owed to creditors that must be paid within a 1-year time frame. Long-term liabilities are any debts owed by the business that are due more than a year out from the current date.

Mortgage not payable is the balance of a mortgage that extends out beyond the current year. For example, you may have paid off 3 years off a 16-year mortgage note, of which the remaining 11 years, not counting the current year, are considered long-term.

Owners' equity is referred to as stockholders' equity. Owners' equity is made up of the initial investment in the business as well as any retained earnings that are reinvested in the business.

Common stock is issued as part of the initial or later-stage investment in the business. Retained earnings are earnings reinvested in the business after the deduction of any distributions to shareholders, such as dividend payments.

Total liabilities and owners' equity comprises all debts and monies that are owed to outside creditors, lenders or banks. This includes remaining monies that are owed to shareholders, including retained earnings invested in the business.

## Conclusion

The balance sheet is the fundamental statement of assets, debts and capital invested in an enterprise.

Before investing in any company, a financier can use the balance sheet to study the following:

- The firm's capability to meet its financial responsibilities
- The amount of funds that has already been invested in the firm
- The company's debt outline
- The category of assets purchased by the enterprise with its financing

It provides an informed and diligent investor an accurate picture of a firm's future performance. This facilitates the creation of informed investment decisions.

# Income Statement

## Concept

This statement highlights an account of sales, expenses and net profit for a given period. It gives operating results for a specific period. It can be described as a financial document showing a company's income and expenses over a given period.

It is also known as an earnings statement or statement of operations. The significance of the income statement is the company's earnings for the period.

Moreover, an income statement can be defined as that statement of a firm that summarizes revenues and expenses over a specified time period. That is, a statement of profit and loss.

It is a financial summary that shows the operating results of a company over a specified period of time, usually 1 year. More specifically, the statement shows a company's revenues, cost and expenses and profits. It breaks down total sales and total expenses.

Income statements are used to find out what areas of business are over budgeted or under budgeted. Specific items that are causing unexpected expenditures can be pinpointed, such as phone, fax, mail and supply costs.

They can also attract monumental increases in cost of goods sold as a percentage of sales. They can also determine income tax liability.

# Features of an Income Statement

## Sales

This figure represents the amount of revenue generated by the business. The amount recorded here is the total sales, less any product returns or sales discounts. Cost of goods sold represents the costs directly associated with making or acquiring products.

Costs include materials purchased from outside suppliers used in the manufacture of a product, as well as any internal expenses directly spent in the manufacturing process. Subtracting cost of goods sold from net sales derives gross profit. It does not include any operating expenses or income taxes.

## Operating Expenses

Operating expenses are daily expenses incurred in the management of a business enterprise and they are categorized into selling and general administrative expenses.

Sales salaries are salaries plus bonuses and commissions paid to sales staff. Collateral and promotions are expenses incurred in the creation of or purchase of printed sales materials used by sales staff in promotion and sales activities.

Promotion fees include any product samples and giveaways used to promote or sell products. Advertising involves creating and placing print or multi-media advertising.

Other sales costs include any other costs associated with selling products. They may include travel, client meals, sales meetings, equipment rental for presentations, copying and miscellaneous printing costs.

Office salaries are salaries of full and part-time office employees. Rents are fees incurred to rent or lease an office or industrial space. Utilities include costs for heating, air conditioning, electricity, and phone equipment and usage used in business activities.

Depreciation is an annual cost that takes into account the loss in value of equipment used in daily administration. An example of equipment that may be subject to depreciation includes copiers, computers, printers and fax machines.

Other overhead costs are expense items that do not fall into other categories or cannot be clearly associated with a particular product or function.

These types of expenses may include insurance, office supplies and cleaning services. Total expenses are a tabulation of all expenses incurred in running a business. This excludes taxes and interest expense on interest income.

Net income before taxes represents the amount of income earned by a business prior to paying income taxes. This figure is arrived at by subtracting total operating expenses from gross profit.

Taxes represent the amount of income taxes you owe to the government and local government. Net income is the amount of the money the business has earned after paying income taxes.

# Statement of Retained Earnings

This is a financial statement that reconciles the balance in retained earnings account at the beginning of the income statement period to the balance at the end of the period.

It can also be described as a statement of all transactions affecting the balance of a company's retained earnings account. Thus, it is the accumulated net income retained for reinvestment in a business, rather than being paid out in dividends to stockholders.

The statement is also known as statement of owners' equity and it explains the change in company's retained earnings over the reporting period.

Retained earnings appears on the balance sheet and is most commonly influenced by income earned by the firm and dividends paid out.

The statement of retained earnings uses information from the income statement and provides information to the balance sheet.

The statement shows the retained earnings at the beginning and end of the accounting period. It is prepared using the following information, beginning retained earnings obtained from a previous statement of retained earnings and net income and dividends paid during the accounting period.

Conclusively, one can emphasize that, a statement of retained earnings shows the changes in the balance of the retained earnings, plus the net income for the period, subtracted by any dividends declared. This computes the ending balance of retained earnings.

# Statement of Cash Flow

It is a financial report that shows incoming and outgoing money during a particular period. This statement can be described as a summary of a company's cash flow over a given period of time.

Moreover, it is also defined as a financial document detailing the exchange of cash between business and the outside world. Various schools of thought categorize this flow as:

- Cash flow from operations the enterprise made by selling goods and services
- Cash flow from financing the company raised by selling shares and bonds

- Cash flow into investing in the company funds spent investing in its future growth

Each of these flows can actually flow both ways. Investors like to see that the company can cover its spending with cash from operations, without having to turn to financing.

The cash flow statement also has to reconcile the net effect of these flows with the difference in its cash holdings at the beginning and end dates of the reporting period.

It is used to analyze the cash inflows and outflows during a designated period of time. It shows whether revenue booked on the income statement has actually been collected.

At the same time, however, remember that the cash flow does not necessarily show all the company's expenses because not all expenses accrued have to be paid right away.

This statement highlights on certain items that are not vividly captured by the income statement. Common examples of these are:

- Large increase in stock purchases

- Increase in debtors value

- Reduction of credit suppliers

- Purchase of equipment and machinery

- Unrecognized stock defects

- Bank's refusal to renew and extend loan

- Total payment of debt

Therefore, the cash flow statement acts like a corporate checkbook that reconciles other financial statements.

# Supplementary Documents

## Notes to Accounts

Notes to accounts are extra information that has to be disclosed to comply with Accounting Standards and the Companies Act in any specific locality.

## Auditors Report

This is a statement from the auditors or accountants that they have examined a business' books of accounts to check whether they have been properly kept. In addition, whether the statements represent a true and fair view of the company's transactions. It is also sometimes referred to as the clean opinion.

It is a section of an annual report containing an accountant's opinion about the accuracy of its financial statement. It can also be described as a report that is recorded in the annual report. It tests to see that an enterprise's financial statements comply with Generally Accepted Accounting Principles (GAAP).

Most auditors' reports consist of three parts. The first states the responsibilities of the auditor and directors. The second is the scope, stating that GAAP was used. Finally the third component gives the auditor's view.

## A Directors' Report

It is a description by the directors of the performance of the business during the accounting period. This also includes various additional disclosures, particularly in relation to directors' shareholdings, remuneration among others.

# SECTION

# B

# Analysis

# Quantitative Ratio Analysis

## *Primary Financial Ratios*

## Short-term Solvency/ Liquidity Ratios

## Concept

This group of ratios provides information about a company's liquidity position. It seeks to determine whether a company can pay its obligations over the short-run without difficulty.

Due to its nature, its primary focus is on the position of current assets and current liabilities.

Liquidity ratios are of utmost interest to short-term stakeholders like short-term creditors, financial institutions and other lenders. The importance of these ratios for these stakeholders cannot be over-emphasized. A thorough understanding of liquidity ratios is essential.

Current assets and current liabilities are basically cash oriented variables. Therefore they change rapidly projecting differing amounts at specific periods of time.

## Current Ratio

This is the most popular and widely used liquidity ratio in financial and business management. It is constructed in the following manner:

**Formula**

**Current Ratio =Current Assets/Current Liabilities**

It is a measure of short-term liquidity. The unit of measurement is either in monetary terms or it is expressed in times. For example if the current ratio is 2.40 times, what does it mean?

It means the specific company has 2.40 dollars in current assets for every 1 dollar in current liabilities. In this scenario the numerator value is greater than the denominator value. We can also say the company has its current liabilities covered 2.40 times over.

Short-term stakeholders like short-term creditors and other lenders prefer a high current ratio. A high current ratio indicates liquidity, that is, the value of the company's current assets exceeds the value of its current liabilities. Nonetheless it may also indicate unproductive use of cash and stock.

A low current ratio, that is, when the numerator value exceeds the denominator value means a firm has liquidity challenges. This means the firm's current liabilities exceed the value of its current assets. A low current ratio may not be a bad sign for an enterprise that has the capacity to borrow a large quantum of financing.

The Industry rule states that the current ratio should be greater or equal to 1. This is because a ratio less than 1 would mean the net working capital is negative thus the firm would face financial distress. This rule is applicable in most types of business concerns.

## Quick Ratio

This ratio is also known as the acid test. Inventory or stock is the primary focus of this ratio. Inventory is the least liquid current asset. The inventory of a firm can become outdated and spoiled.

A large amount of inventory is a clear sign of an enterprise that will face liquidity problems in the short-run. This is because a firm may have its working capital absorbed by slow-moving inventory.

In order to calculate pure liquidity, inventory is removed. Quick ratio is constructed in the following manner:

**Formula**

**Quick Ratio =Current Assets- Inventory/Current Liabilities**

This ratio is a measure of short-run liquidity. It goes a step further by omitting inventory in order to extract the true status of a firm's liquidity position.

For example if the quick ratio is 0.60, what does it mean? It means that the enterprise has liquidity problems because its current liabilities exceed its current assets.

This is probably due to the impact of its inventory on the current assets value. It may be that the specific firm's inventory account for about 50% or more of its current assets.

It is important to note that stock or inventory is not as liquid as cash. If a firm's inventory constitutes a large mass of slow-moving products then the firm will face serious cash shortages.

## Cash Ratio

This ratio measures the relationship between cash and a firm's current liabilities. It is a short-term liquidity measure. Most short-term stakeholders like short-term creditors or lenders will be interested in a firm's cash ratio.

It is constructed in the following manner:

**Formula**

**Cash Ratio =Cash /Current Liabilities**

This ratio is also a measure of a firm's liquidity position. The focus is on the firm's cash value. The cash value is the most liquid asset of a firm.

This ratio helps to determine an accurate picture of a company's liquidity position and standing. For example if the cash ratio is 2.20, what does it mean?

It means that the value of the firm's cash in hand and at bank exceeds the value of its current liabilities 2.20 times over. It also means the company has 2.20 dollars in cash for every 1 dollar in current liabilities.

Since the numerator value far exceeds the denominator value, the firm has a good liquidity status and is experiencing financial relief.

# Net Working Capital to Total Assets

This ratio measures the correlation between working capital and a firm's total asset base. Net working capital is the difference between current assets and current liabilities of an enterprise.

Working capital is the quantum of money that is used for the day to day administration of the firm. It is seen as the amount of short-term liquidity a firm has.

It is measured in the following manner:

**Formula**

**Net working capital to total assets =Net working capital /Total Assets**

The difference between the firm's current asset and liabilities reveals the value of financing available for current expenditure. It also unveils the degree of liquidity of the specific firm.

Therefore, a positive and ideal situation is when the net working capital exceeds the total assets. So, if the net working capital to total assets ratio is 5.5, what does it mean?

It means the firm has 5.5 dollars for every dollar of total assets. It also means the firm's total assets are covered 5.5 times over. If the value was less than 0, then it means the company has low levels of liquidity and is in danger of becoming financially distressed.

## Interval Measure

This ratio measures the relationship between a firm's current assets and its average daily operating costs. Average daily operating costs are the variable costs that accrue to a firm due to daily transactions.

The firm needs a constant flow of financing in order to cater for these costs. Therefore it is imperative that the firm has enough current assets to cover its daily operating costs.

This ratio is calculated in the following manner:

**Formula**

**Interval measure =Current assets /Average daily operating costs**

This formula reveals the capacity of a firm to keep going during crisis situations that affect cash inflows.

During these times, the interval measure is used to determine the ability of the firm to cover its costs with the absence of inflows. For instance when the interval measure is 30 days, what does it mean?

It means the ability of the firm to cover its operating cash flow is a 1-month interval. This means the value of the firm's current assets covers the value of the firm's operating costs for a month.

Industry rule states that a firm's current assets should cover its operating costs at least for three months. That is, it should cover its operating costs at least 3 months over.

## Asset Management/ Turnover Ratios

## Concept

Asset management or turnover ratios measure the efficiency at which a firm utilizes its assets. This measure is sometimes referred to as asset use ratios.

These ratios are also described as turnover because they measure the degree to which assets can be transformed into sales. Therefore it is important to note that we shall be dealing with formulae that describe how intensively a firm uses its assets to generate sales.

## Inventory Turnover ratio

These measures highlight the correlation between cost of goods sold and average stock or inventory.

In some circumstances it will be more useful to use sales instead of cost of goods sold. Cost of goods sold is the costs that accrue to the firm during sales transactions.

Average inventory is the addition of the beginning value and the ending value divided by two. Average inventory is often used during calculations of inventory turnover but there is no hard and fast rule.

It all depends on the purpose of the calculation. Sometimes certain circumstances require the use of the ending value. Inventory turnover is calculated in the following manner:

**Formula**

**Inventory turnover =Cost of goods sold or sales/ average inventory or inventory**

The formula measures the efficiency at which the firm sells of its inventory or turns over its inventory. The higher this ratio the more efficiently we measure inventory. The numerator value should exceed the denominator value.

This shows that the firm generates a specific amount of sales per dollar of inventory. For example if the inventory turnover ratio is 4.0 times, what does it mean?

It means the firm sold off or turned over its entire inventory 4.0 times over during the year. It also means the firm generated 4.0 dollars from every dollar of inventory.

The firm utilizes its inventory so efficiently it generates sales that cover its inventory 4 times over. The Industry rule states that the numerator value should always exceed the denominator value by a ratio of 2:1.

## Age of Inventory ratio

This ratio measures the amount of days on average inventory remains in stock. It highlights how long it takes to turn over inventory on average. It is also known as the Days' sales in inventory.

Age of inventory is calculated in the following manner:

### Formula

**Age of Inventory =365 days/ inventory turnover**

This ratio measures how long inventory takes to be sold. The number of days should be close to the industry average.

The figure should not be too low because it could lead to stock-outs due to the lack of inventory. If the figure is too high, a firm will accumulate excessive inventory which causes waste in monetary terms.

For example if the age of inventory of the firm is 200 days what does it mean? It means the inventory of the specific firm stays on the shelf for 200 days on average before it is sold.

This means the firm has 200 days supply of stock. It can also be described as having 200 days of sales in inventory.

## Receivables Turnover ratio

This ratio is used to determine the speed at which a business retrieves its credit sales. This ratio analyses the relationship between sales and accounts receivables or debtors. This measurement seeks to establish the number of times we collected our credit sales and reloaned it.

Receivables turnover ratio is measured in the following manner:

**Formula**

**Receivables turnover=Sales/ accounts receivable**

From the above formula, it is clear that it is defined in the same way as inventory turnover. This ratio seeks to derive the number of times a firm is able to collect its outstanding credits and utilize those credits for profit purposes. The suitability of this measure is determined by comparison to the industry average.

For instance if the receivables turnover is 15 times, what does it mean? It means the specific firm under analysis collected or retrieved its outstanding debtors and reloaned the money 15 times during the course of the year. Preferably the value of the numerator should exceed the value of the denominator.

## Average Collection Period ratio

This ratio measures in average days the amount of time it takes to collect credit sales. This ratio measures the amount of days on average debtors' remains uncollected. It is also known as the days' sales in receivables and age of receivables.

Average Collection period is constructed in the following manner:

**Formula**

**Average collection period =365 days/ receivables turnover**

Average collection period highlights the value of sales currently uncollected. It gives more meaning to the receivables turnover ratio because of the conversion to days.

If the days' sales in receivables happen to be 60 days, what does it mean? It means that on average this specific firm collects its credit sales in 60 days. It can also be described as having 60 days' worth of sales currently in the hands of debtors.

Determining a suitable ratio will depend on the industry average. It is preferable if the outcome is close to the industry average.

## Payables Turnover ratio

This ratio determines the length of time it takes for a specific business to pay its bills. This measurement focuses on the average period of time. It highlights the relationship between the cost of goods sold and accounts payable. The assumption is that firms purchase all their goods and services on credit.

Payables Turnover is measured in the following manner:

**Formula**

**Payables Turnover = Cost of goods sold/ accounts payable**

This ratio seeks to determine the frequency in which a firm settles its day to day expenditure. The standard output of this measure depends on the industry average. Ideally, this ratio should be close to the industry average.

If the ratio is 5.0 times, what does it mean? It means the business averagely pays its outstanding bills 5.0 times during the course of the year. The numerator value should exceed the denominator value.

## Age of Payables

This ratio indicates how long averagely it takes a business to pay its suppliers. It is measured in days. It assumes that the majority of accounts payable results from the purchase of materials for resale.

It is also known as the days' sales in payables. It weighs the relationship between 365 days and the payables turnover value.

It is defined and measured in the following manner:

**Formula**

**Age of Turnover =365 days/ payables turnover**

This ratio portrays the number of days it takes for a company to settle its bills on average. So if the age of turnover is 100 days, what does it mean? It means the firm on average takes 100 days to pay its accounts payables.

This measure should be close to the industry average. It should be on the high side if possible. If the ratio is too low, the firm can obtain short-term financing by taking longer to pay. Alternatively, if the ratio is too high it can establish a reputation and the specific firm can get its credit privileges cut off.

## Net Working Capital Turnover

This ratio measures the intensity of sales value a firm can derive from its net working capital. Similarly, it measures the amount of sales dollars earned for every dollar of net working capital. It establishes the relationship between sales and net working capital.

It is constructed in the following manner:

### Formula

### NWC Turnover =Sales/ Net working capital

The ratio measures how useful the net working capital is to the specific business. So if the NWC turnover is 20 times, what does it mean?

It means the sales value covers the net working capital 20 times over. It can also be interpreted as every dollar of net working capital earns 20 dollars of sales.

A high ratio is the desired trend. A very low ratio indicates excess cash that should be utilized in a more efficient, effective and timely manner. This ratio must be as close as possible to the industry average.

## Fixed Asset Turnover

This ratio measures the quantum of sales dollars that are earned for every dollar of fixed assets. It also highlights the number of times sales covers net fixed assets. It measures the relationship between sales and net fixed assets.

Fixed asset turnover is measured in the following manner:

**Formula**

**Fixed asset Turnover =Sales/ Net fixed assets**

This ratio indicates how useful the fixed assets are to the efficient running of the business.

So if the fixed asset turnover ratio is 0.9 times, what does it mean? It means for every dollar in net fixed assets, the firm generated 0.9 dollars in sales. Similarly, it can also mean that the sales value covers the fixed asset value 0.9 times. This shows that the denominator value exceeds the numerator value.

A high ratio is a desirable trend. A very low ratio indicates excess assets that should be disposed of. Alternatively, a very high ratio may indicate that assets are old and need replacing.

## Total Asset Turnover

This ratio measures the amount of times sales covers the total asset value. It measures the degree in dollar terms at which sales is generated for every dollar in total assets. Total asset turnover focuses on the relationship between sales and total assets.

It is constructed and defined in the following manner:

### Formula

### Total asset Turnover =Sales/ Total assets

This ratio is a reflection of the usefulness of total assets to the running of the specific firm under analysis. So if the total asset turnover is 0.7 times, what does it mean?

It means the value of sales covers the value of total fixed assets 0.7 times over during the course of the year.

It also means for every dollar in total assets, the firm generates 0.7 dollars in sales. Notice that the denominator value exceeds the numerator value. A high ratio is the desired trend.

A very low ratio means useless assets should be sold. Extremely high ratios may mean that there is a shortage of assets and the firm is not optimizing its opportunities.

## Long-Term Solvency/ Debt Management ratios

## Concept

Long-term solvency ratios measure a firm's ability to settle its long-term obligations or debt. It indicates a firm's financial leverage or gearing.

They are known as leverage ratios. These ratios measure the balance between debt and equity. The analysis of these ratios highlights the degree of stability of the specific business concern.

# Total Debt ratio

This ratio measures the quantum of all forms of debt that is utilized by a business for administrative and other purposes. It highlights the percentage of debt in the firm's capital structure. A firm's capital structure is an addition of its equity value and its debt value.

The total debt ratio is a relationship between the difference between a firm's total assets and total equity value divided by its total assets value.

It is constructed or formulated in the following manner:

**Formula**

**Total debt ratio =Total assets- Total equity/ Total assets**

This ratio measures the percentage and degree of debt in monetary terms that a specific firm utilizes. Therefore if the total debt ratio of a firm is 35%, what does it mean? It means that the specific firm under review utilizes or uses 35% debt.

It may also be interpreted as the enterprise having 0.35 dollars in debt for every 1 dollar in assets. In this instance the denominator value exceeds the numerator value. The interpretation of its output depends on whether or not the make-up of the capital structure matters.

## Debt/ Equity ratio

This ratio measures the proportion of debt and equity in a company's capital structure. It measures in terms of percentage and times the relationship between a firm's debt value and its equity value. Debt/ Equity ratio is a primary variation of the total debt ratio.

This ratio is formulated in the following manner:

### Formula

**Debt/ Equity ratio =Total debt/ Total equity**

The above formula describes the correlation between a company's debt value and its equity value. It seeks to ascertain the degree of debt and equity a specific firm uses, which is the makeup of its capital structure. For instance if the debt/ equity ratio of a firm is 0.45 times, what does it mean?

It means the total debt value of the firm covers the total debt value 0.45 times over. It may also be interpreted as the firm having 0.45 dollars debt in every 1 dollar of equity. This means the equity value exceeds the debt value. This ratio is an important financial leverage measure.

## Equity Multiplier

This ratio determines the correlation between a firm's total assets and its total equity value. It is an important variation of the total debt ratio and it is closely related to the debt/ equity ratio. It ascertains the relationship between a company's asset value and its equity value.

It is measured in the following manner:

**Formula**

**Equity multiplier =Total assets/ Total equity**

The equity multiplier measures in percentage and times the total assets value in terms of the stockholder's value. It is 1+ the debt/ equity ratio. So if the equity multiplier is 2 times, what does it mean? It means the total asset value covers the total equity value 2 times over.

It may also be interpreted as the company having 2 dollars in total assets for every 1 dollar in total equity. In this instance the numerator value exceeds the denominator value. This measure is an important measure of a firm's financial leverage or gearing.

## Long-term Debt ratio

This ratio measure a firm's total capitalization in terms of its total asset value. The long-term debt ratio is an important measure because it is more stable measure of debt. The short-term debt of a firm is always changing and thus it's unstable. Therefore financial analysts are more interested in a firm's long-term debt.

This intriguing ratio is constructed in the following manner:

**Formula**

**Long-term debt ratio =Long-term debt/ Long-term debt +Total equity**

This ratio measures the relationship between a firm's long-term debt and total equity. It is known as a firm's total capitalization value. The financial manager and any student of business should focus his attention on this specific value.

For example if the long-term debt ratio is 0.30 times, what does it mean? It means for every 0.30 dollars in long-term debt the firm under review has 1 dollar in equity.

Another interpretation would be that the firm has its total equity value covered 0.30 times over. This means its denominator value exceeds its numerator value.

## Interest Coverage ratio

This ratio is an important measure of long-term solvency. It measures the relationship between interest obligations and pre-tax income. Interest coverage ratio is also known as times interest earned ratio.

This ratio is formulated in the following manner:

### Formula

### Interest coverage ratio =EBIT/ Interest

This ratio measures how efficiently a company has its interest obligations covered. For instance if the interest coverage ratio is 6 times, what does it mean?

This means the firm's interest obligations are covered 6 times over. It may also be interpreted as the firm having 6 dollars in pre-tax income for every 1 dollar of interest obligations.

## Cash Coverage ratio

This ratio measures the quantum or degree at which cash can be generated from the operations of a firm. It determines the relationship between earnings before depreciation, interest, and taxes and the interest expense.

This ratio is formulated in the following manner:

**Formula**

**Cash coverage ratio =EBDIT/ Interest**

This measure ascertains the EBDIT-EBIT+ depreciation and its impact on interest obligations of a company. It is also used as a measure of cash flow available to meet operational financial obligations.

For example if the cash coverage ratio is 8 times, what does it mean? It means the firm has its interest bill covered 8 times over. It also means for every 1 dollars of interest, the firm has 8 dollars of income generated.

## Profitability Ratios

## Concept

These ratios are the most popular type of financial ratios. They are used extensively to determine how profitable a particular venture is.

In order to ascertain the profit margins of a specific firm, it is dependant on the efficient use of a firm's assets and the efficient nature of a firm's operations.

## Cost of Goods Sold to Sales ratio

This ratio measures the cost of goods (COGS) sold relative to sales. It helps ascertain the value of a firm's inputs. That is, it helps determine a company's cost structure and its impact on the profit levels of a firm.

It is formulated in the following manner:

**Formula**

**COGS to Sales=COGS/ Sales×100**

This ratio measures the percentage of COGS in terms of sales. So if the COGS to sales value is 30%, what does it mean? It means the firm has a 30% proportion of COGS in sales.

It may also be interpreted as the firm having a 30% cost factor in the ultimate sales value. The standard measure for this ratio is determined by final value. The desired trend is the lower the ratio, the lower the cost value.

## Gross Profit to Sales ratio

This ratio measures the amount of gross profit that makes up sales. It highlights on the relationship between gross profit and sales. This ratio is an important measure for companies because it determines their profit margins.

Gross Profit to sales ratio is formulated in the following manner:

**Formula**

**Gross Profit to Sales=Gross profit/ Sales×100**

This measure helps to ascertain the amount of money a firm generates in terms of gross profit from sales.

So if the gross profit to sales value is 20%, what does it mean? It means the company under analysis generates 0.20 dollars in profit for every 1 dollar in sales.

It may also be interpreted as the firm's gross profit constitutes 20% of its total sales value. The desired trend is the higher the ratio, the higher the percentage of profit obtained.

## Operating Expenses to Sales ratio

This ratio measures the proportion of operating expenses in the sales structure of a firm.

It portrays the relationship between operating expenses and sales. This ratio helps a firm to determine the impact of a firm's operating costs on its net sales value.

This highly important ratio is constructed in the following manner:

**Formula**

**Operating expenses to Net sales=Operating expenses/ Net sales×100**

It is a very important ratio because it highlights the firm's expense structure relative to its sales and its attendant impact. For instance if the operating expenses to net sales ratio is 25%, what does it mean?

It means the company generates 0.25 dollars of expenses for every 1 dollar of sales. It also means the company has a 25% cost bill relative to its net sales. A firm's desired trend would be the lower the ratio, the lower expenses relative to sales.

## Net Income to Sales ratio

This ratio highlights on the proportion of net income earned on every sales dollar. It crystallizes the relationship between net income and net sales. This ratio is a very important measure of profitability because it deals with the bottom line that is the net income.

It is formulated in the following manner:

**Formula**

**Net income to Net sales=Net income/ Net sales×100**

This ratio is the ultimate measure of profitability in any going concern or business. So if the net income to net sales ratio is 15%, what does it mean? It means in accounting terms, the firm generates 0.15 dollars in profit for every 1 dollar in net sales.

It also means the profit margin constitutes 15% of the total net sales value. In normal practice it is desirable if the ratio is high. That is, the higher the ratio, the more profitable each sale.

## Return on Assets ratio

This ratio measures the quantum of returns that a firm's fixed assets are generating. It is also a measure of profit relative to every dollar of assets. It determines the relationship between a firm's net income and average total assets.

It can be formulated in the following manner:

**Formula**

**Return on assets=Net income/ Average total assets**

Return on assets helps businesses determine the value of its profit per dollar of its average total assets. It also helps to decipher the efficiency of a firm's assets in terms of their impact on return or income.

The desired trend for business ventures are a high ratio. The higher the ratio, the higher the return means the company under review utilizes its fixed assets efficiently.

## Return on Equity ratio

It is a measure of how the shareholders performed during the course of the financial year. It determines the relationship between net income and average shareholder's equity. This ratio is the ultimate measure of performance. It is sometimes called return on net worth.

It is constructed in the following manner:

**Formula**

**Return on Equity=Net income/ Average shareholder's equity**

This measure is affected by 3 important variables. These are operating efficiency, asset use efficiency and financial leverage. This is known as the Du Pont Identity.

The breakdown of return on equity helps financial managers to approach financial statement analysis in a systematic and effective manner. If the return on equity ratio is 20%, what does it mean?

It means the firm under analysis generated 0.20 dollars in profit per every dollar of average equity.

Return on equity may also be measured as return on assets multiplied by equity multiplier. The desired trend is a high ratio.

That is, the higher the return on equity ratio, the happier and more content shareholders or owners would become. If the return on equity exceeds the return on assets it highlights the firm's gearing structure.

# Stock Market Measures

## Concept

This group of measures is ascertained by the value of the market price per share. These measures are important for publicly listed enterprises. Information for the effective use of this measure is not necessarily derived from financial statements because they are market value ratios.

## Price/ Earnings ratio

This ratio measures the relationship between price per share and earnings per share. The earning per share is defined as the division between net income and shares outstanding. Price/ earnings ratio measures how much investor's are willing to pay per dollar of current earnings.

It is formulated in the following manner:

**Formula**

**Price/ Earnings ratio=Price per share/ Earnings per share**

This ratio measures the amount of times a venture shares sell relative to earnings. It also highlights the price/ earning multiple. This multiple is derived from the correlation between price per share and earnings per share.

So if the price earnings ratio is 10 times, what does it mean? It means the shares of the specific firm under review sell 10 times earnings. It can also be interpreted as the firm having a P/E multiple of 10.

A high P/E multiple is usually interpreted as a positive development because it reveals on hindsight that the firm has significant prospects for future growth and development.

## Market to Book ratio

Market to book ratio facilitates the efficient determination of the market value of a firm's investments to their cost. It highlights the correlation between a firm's market value per share and its book value per share. The book value of a firm is its total equity divided by the number of shares outstanding.

This market value measure is formulated in the following manner:

**Formula**

**Market to Book ratio=Market value per share/ Book value per share**

This ratio is an important measure of a shares market value. For instance if the market to book value of a company is 3 times, what does it mean? It means the firm's market value per share covers its book value per share 3 times over.

It may also mean that for every 1 dollar book value per share, the firm generates 3 dollars market value per share.

## Corporate Growth Ratios

## Concept

These ratios measure improvements or decline in performance from year to year. These measures constitute profit growth, asset growth and sales growth.

Corporate growth ratios are an important determinant of corporate performance and sustainability.

## Profit Growth ratio

These ratios measure the quantum of profit that has increased or decreased during two operational periods. It highlights on the relationship between change in profit and beginning profit.

This specific ratio is constructed in the following manner:

**Formula**

**Profit Growth ratio=Profit (yr2)-Profit (yr1) /**

**Profit (yr1)**

This ratio clearly shows the changes in profit and its impact on the profit growth of a firm. For instance if the profit growth is 0.30 times, what does it mean? It means the profit has grown by 30% during the course of the financial year.

It also means the change in profit covers the beginning profit value 0.30 times. In this instance the denominator value exceeds the numerator value.

A high value is the desired standard. That is, the higher the ratio, the higher the growth in profit which is a desirable outcome.

## Sales Growth ratio

This ratio measures the degree of increase or decrease in sales over a period of time. It portrays the correlation between change in sales and beginning sales value.

The sales growth ratio is formulated in the following manner:

**Formula**

**Sales Growth ratio=Sales (yr2)-Sales (yr1) / Sales (yr1)**

This ratio highlights the changes in sales and its impact on corporate performance. For instance if the sales growth is 0.70 times, what does it mean? It means the sales have increased by 70% during the course of the operational year.

It also interpreted as the change in sales covering the beginning sales value 0.70 times. The denominator value exceeds the numerator value.

A high value is the desired standard as long it is proportional to profit growth. If sales growth increases but profit declines then the additional sales could be harmful.

## Asset Growth ratio

This ratio measures improvements or decline in asset performance from year to year. This ratio measures the quantum of increase or decrease in assets over a specific operational period.

Asset growth ratio is formulated in the following manner:

**Formula**

**Asset Growth ratio=Asset (yr2)-Asset (yr1) / Asset (yr1)**

This ratio defines the changes in asset values and its attendant impact on corporate growth and development. So, if the asset growth is 0.50 times, what does it mean? It means the asset value have increased by 50% during the course of the period.

Another interpretation is that, the change in asset value covers the beginning asset value 0.50 times. The denominator value exceeds the numerator value in this specific case.

The desired standard is a situation where the asset growth should be proportional to sales and profit growth.

## Internal and Sustainable Growth Ratios

### Concept

These ratios are an important tool for long-term financial planning. These ratios highlight the relationship between corporate growth and external financing.

Internal growth ratio measures the extent of growth without the use of external financing. Sustainable growth ratio measures the maximum growth rate of a firm without the use of external equity financing while maintaining a standard debt/ equity ratio.

## Internal Growth Ratio

Internal growth ratio highlights the maximum growth rate that a firm can achieve without external financing sources. This ratio reveals the growth rate at which a firm can continue its operations with internal financing sources.

It is constructed in the following manner:

**Formula**

**Internal Growth Ratio=ROA× b / 1-ROA× b**

**b= Retention ratio= addition to retained earnings / Net income**

**ROA= Return on assets= Net income/ Total assets**

This ratio shows the correlation between return on assets and the plowback profit. These two variables help to determine the maximum growth rate of the firm when it utilizes its internal financing sources only.

So if the internal growth ratio of the firm is 15%, what does it mean? It means the specific firm under analysis can expand at a maximum rate of 15% per year without the use of external financing.

## Sustainable Growth Ratio

This ratio measures the maximum growth rate a company can attain without the use of external equity financing while maintaining a constant debt/ equity situation. It is the maximum growth margin an enterprise can maintain without increasing its financial leverage.

Sustainable growth ratio is formulated in the following manner:

**Formula**

**Sustainable Growth Ratio=ROE× b / 1-ROE× b**

**b= Retention ratio= addition to retained earnings / Net income**

**ROA= Return on equity= Net income/ Total equity**

This ratio shows the relationship between return on equity and the plowback profit. These two variables facilitate the determination of the maximum growth rate of the firm without external equity financing.

For instance, if the sustainable growth ratio of the firm is 35%, what does it mean? It means the specific firm under analysis can expand at a maximum rate of 35% per year without utilizing external equity financing.

# Qualitative Ratio Analysis

**Concept**

Qualitative analysis uses subjective judgment based on non-quantifiable information to determine pertinent conclusions about a company. This method of analysis is different from quantitative analysis, which focuses on numbers.

However, these two techniques should be used together in order to achieve total quality financial analysis of a business concern.

Qualitative factors are an indelible part of a company. They represent a negative or positive power. Supplementing quantitative analysis with qualitative analysis increases insight into the specific company under review.

This study often gives analysts a clearer and factual picture since certain key elements, such as managerial competency and employee relations, does not show up in quantitative examination.

In conclusion, qualitative analysis is the process of analyzing the qualities of a firm in order to determine whether these qualities have a positive, negative or minimal outcome on the performance of a company.

These qualities include management competency, industry cycle variations, research and development and labor relationships.

The conclusion of a qualitative ratio analysis either confirms or raises issues about the findings of the quantitative ratio assessment.

## Management

It is imperative that while conducting an analysis of an enterprise, the level of management expertise should be looked at critically. All organizations benefit tremendously from a well-organized management set-up where authority and responsibility are clearly defined.

It is therefore essential for companies to have multi-skilled management teams that consistently seek to create and innovate. An analyst must discern whether management is focused,target-driven and competent.

Management is the primary carrier of the corporate vision, so they must exhibit effective, efficient and timely decision-making skills.

## Industry

Every industry has a specific and periodic life-span. It is important to realize that every business concern is located in an industry and is affected by the tremors and earthquakes of that industry.

Therefore industry cycle variations and changes should be analyzed in order to determine the type of effects they would have on the performance of a firm in that industry.

Industry cycles could either have a positive, negative or minimal effect on the performance of a company. A proactive company should be able to take advantage of industry cycles in order to leapfrog and attain an indelible competitive advantage.

## Research and Development

In contemporary business times, the strength of a firm's research and development unit is a premium asset. Investment in research and development leads to an incremental growth in every company.

While conducting financial analysis, the analyst must ascertain the degree of research and development in the specific company under analysis. The strength of an enterprises research capability is an enviable corporate quality.

Research and development helps position a company positively. It harnesses the strengths of the enterprise and gives it sustainable competitive advantage over its rivals. Research findings facilitate extraordinary strategic maneuvers.

## Labor Relations

Labor is the lifeblood of every organization. Without labor all organizations would run to a halt. The importance of cordial labor relations in companies cannot be underscored.

An important measure of the strength of contemporary businesses is the extent of human capital investment. Every proactive and futuristic company should seek to develop a productive relationship with its employees. This will help offset continuous negative setbacks.

Analysts must determine the degree of skills enhancement, opportunities for career growth, extrinsic and intrinsic benefits and interpersonal fluidity of the specific enterprise under review. Excellent labor relations and highly skilled employees magnify the inherent competencies of every business.

# SECTION

# C

# Conclusion

# Vandyck's Financial Analysis Continuum

**Concept**

**Vandyck's Financial Analysis Continuum** is the optimum mix of a company's quantitative ratio investigation decisions and its qualitative ratio examination decisions in order to originate total quality financial decisions.

This innovative concept is illustrated below:

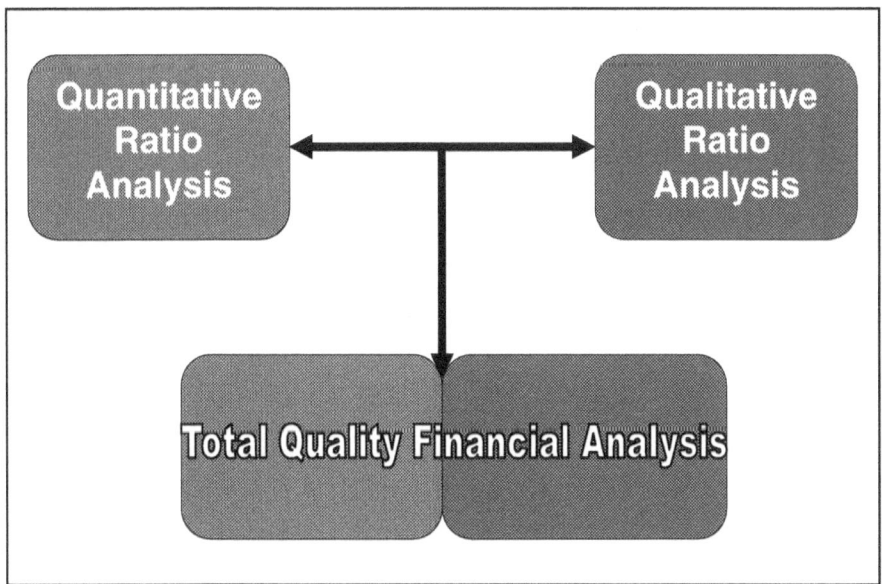

Every company seeks to accomplish its financial objectives and targets within a specific time frame. **Vandyck's Financial Analysis Continuum** involves certain laid out procedures that make possible the accomplishment of strategic financial goals. These actions are:

- The detection of key ratios needed for the precise case taking into consideration the cash flow statement.

- Consideration of past performance indices, industry trends and the importance and usefulness of the particular case under investigation.

- Formulation of calculations while avoiding out of date figures and worthless numbers.

- Determination of outcomes by considering the fit between qualitative and quantitative factors.

- Adjusting and controlling by taking corrective actions if the need arises.

# Total Quality Power Points

❖ A ratio can be high or low depending on the specific scenario. A ratio is high because the numerator value is high or the denominator value is low. A ratio is low because the numerator value is low or the denominator value is high.

❖ During interpretation, the analyst should determine which part of the fraction is the principal cause of the value being high or low.

❖ Finally, these values would then be compared to the qualities of the company in order to derive total quality financial decisions. Total quality decisions create sustainable competitive advantage and incredible business growth.

# Total Quality Power Quotes

❖ Financial education needs to become a part of our national curriculum and scoring systems so that it's not just the rich kids that learn about money… it's all of us. **(David Bach)**

❖ In financial management, the quality of a solution depends on the potency of the technique. **(Charles K. Vandyck)**

❖ Before you can really start setting financial goals, you need to determine where you stand financially. **(David Bach)**

❖ It has been my experience that competency in mathematics, both in numerical manipulations and in understanding its conceptual foundations, enhances a person's ability to handle the more ambiguous and qualitative relationships that dominate our day-to-day financial decision-making. **(Alan Greenspan)**

❖ A big part of financial freedom is having your heart and mind free from worry about the what-ifs of life. **(Suze Orman)**

❖ To succeed, you will soon learn, as I did, the importance of a solid foundation in the basics of education—literacy, both verbal and numerical, and communication skills. **(Alan Greenspan)**

❖ The most important thing for an accounting professional is to make numbers an integral part of daily activities. **(Natasha L. Jones)**

# Published Books

- Let Go Of Fear: Let In Unconditional Love (2006, Trafford Publishing Ltd.)

- Transcending The Norm: A Collection Of Enchanting Poetic Verses (2006, Trafford Publishing Ltd.)

# Upcoming Book

- The Art Of Proposal Writing: Transforming Ideas Into Profitable Activities